This book belongs to:

....

About this book

This *Letterland ABC Book* takes you and your child to the imaginary world of Letterland where letters come to life. Each page introduces a new Letterland character and repeats the character's letter sound at the start of many words. Have fun emphasising the sound again and again as you read it aloud and look for key objects. You can check the Word List at the back of the book to see how many you have spotted.

Children love to learn this secret Letterland trick for discovering letter sounds: just START to say any Letterlander's name. The very first sound that comes out of your mouth is the sound their letter usually makes in words!

The Letterland System teaches all 44 letter sounds in the English language – not just the sounds of the alphabet – through stories rather than rules. When you have met all the alphabet characters in this *ABC book* you might like to learn some of the stories that explain other sounds and many other spelling patterns in the English language, for example **sh** as in **sh**e in *Beyond ABC*, and **ir** as in f**ir**st in *Far Beyond ABC*.

Published by Letterland International Ltd
Barton, Cambridge, CB23 7AY, UK

LETTERLAND® is a registered trade mark of Lyn Wendon.

The authors assert the moral right to be identified as the authors of this work. All rights reserved. No part of this publication may be reproduced, stored in a retrieval system, or transmitted in any form or by any means, electronic, mechanical, photocopying, recording or otherwise, without either the prior permission of the Publisher or a licence permitting restricted copying in the United Kingdom issued by the Copyright Licensing Agency Ltd, 90 Tottenham Court Road,

London W1T 4LP. This book is sold subject to the condition that it shall not by way of trade or otherwise be lent, hired out or otherwise circulated without the Publisher's prior consent.
British Library Cataloguing in Publication Data. A catalogue record for this book is available from the British Library.

Written by Lyn Wendon, Domenica de Rosa & Lisa Holt
Illustrated by Geri Livingston
Design by Mike Watts & Lisa Holt

Printed in Singapore

Letterland®

ABC

Written by Lyn Wendon, Domenica de Rosa & Lisa Holt

Illustrated by Geri Livingston

Based on characters originated by Lyn Wendon.

Welcome to Letterland

You may think that letters are just black lines and curves in rows on a page. If so, it's time to think again.

The people and animals in Letterland usually hide behind their plain black letter shapes. Fortunately, in this book you can look into their secret land and see what they are really like!

You'll meet Annie Apple, Bouncy Ben, Clever Cat and lots more – including one or two trouble-makers like Red Robot and Walter Walrus!

Are you ready?
Let's go!

Welcome to Letterland

Annie Apple is a very important talking apple because she knows how to appear in words and make a special sound in them. It's the same sound you can hear at the start of her name, 'ă'.

Annie Apple lives in an apple orchard in Letterland. She has lots of animal friends. Can you see an anteater, an alligator and an antelope? She also has other amazing visitors. Sometimes an acrobat swings by or an astronaut drops in! The only visitors Annie doesn't like are the ants when they tickle her.

Mr A, the Apron Man, looks after all the Letterland apples. He gathers the talking apples in his apron. Can you see Annie on an applestand at the top of this page?

Annie Apple   ant   arrow   acrobat

Here's Bouncy Ben. He is a very happy bunny rabbit, always having fun with his brothers in their blue boat. Can you see another brother far away in a hot-air balloon?

Ben has a bouncy ball, too. Sometimes he balances his ball on top of his head, between his big, brown ears. Can you see him at the top of this page? He must be very good at balancing to keep it there!

Bunnies love to bounce and Ben is the best bouncer in Letterland. He makes a special sound as he bounces about in words. Can you guess what it is? Listen to the 'b…' sound at the start of his name and then you'll have his special sound.

Bouncy Ben   bat   ball   boat

Clever Cat loves to sit by the Letterland castle, having a cup of cocoa and doing her crossword puzzle. She is such a clever cat she can fill in all the words before she has finished her cake!

If you went to Letterland you would probably see Clever Cat driving around in her car. If anyone has a problem, Clever Cat will come to help. She knows how to cook carrots and cauliflower and make custard and cakes. She knows how to count, how to clean her car, how to carry things carefully and lots more!

If anyone in Letterland asks, "Who can help us with this problem?" the answer is usually: "Clever Cat can!"

Clever   Cat   cup   cake   cow

Dippy Duck lives by the Letterland duckpond. Can you see her specially shaped Duck Door?

Everyone loves the duckpond. Dogs, deer and donkeys come to drink and dip their feet in the water. They also come to the duckpond to watch Dippy Duck diving down deep.

When Dippy isn't splashing and diving in her duckpond she loves to draw. Can you see anything in the distance you think she might like to draw? Do you think the dinosaur could be a *real* dinosaur?

Dippy Duck doesn't quack like other ducks. She's a Letterland duck so she makes a short little 'd…' sound instead!

Dippy Duck   dog   doll   donkey

E e

Eddy Elephant is having an exciting time at the Letterland fair. He is trying a new trick to show everybody – juggling eggs! He isn't exactly an expert yet, but he keeps on trying.

Can you see Mr E, the Easy Magic Man, standing under the Entrance sign on that big tent? He showed Eddy Elephant the juggling trick. He also showed Eddy some tricks for him to do in words. Eddy especially enjoys making his sound at the start of the word elephant!

Eddy Elephant also has a clever Elephant-on-End trick. Can you see him doing that trick at the top of this page? Can you find an emerald ring in the big picture?

Eddy Elephant   eggs   Entrance   EXIT

Help! There is a fire in the Letterland forest. Never fear, Firefighter Fred is here to put out the flames.

Firefighter Fred is famous in Letterland for putting out fires in a flash. Whenever there is a fire, he rushes to help. Firefighter Fred also comes to the Letterland school and talks to the children about the dangers of fire and how to keep safe. He tells them never to play with matches or fireworks. Then he lets them climb on to his fire engine. Firefighter Fred will have this fire out in a flash, too. Listen to the sound he makes when he's fighting fires with foam, 'fff…fff…fff…'!

Can you see which animals are running away from the fire? How many frogs can you see?

Firefighter Fred   frogs   fox   farm

Let's meet Golden Girl in her garden. Golden Girl loves to play in her garden, and swing on her own swing. She loves gardening, too – in fact, her grandma and grandpa think she is so good at gardening that they sometimes call her 'Green Girl'.

Golden Girl grows all sorts of good things in her garden. She has a greenhouse too, where she grows glorious green grapes. Look out, Golden Girl! Your goat may be eating grass now, but I bet he knows how good your green grapes are.

When Golden Girl isn't in her garden, she loves going around Letterland in her special Go-Cart. Can you see her driving it at the top of the page?

Golden Girl   garden   goat   grapes

Halfway up a high hill in Letterland is Harry Hat Man's House. In his house, he has a Hat Shop where he makes hundreds of hats. He even made a hat for his house when the roof blew off!

If you want to buy a hat, please ask Harry very quietly. Why? Because he hates noise. That's why you can hardly hear him when he whispers his sound: 'hhh…'. He doesn't even wear shoes because they make too much noise as he hops along.

When Harry Hat Man feels especially happy, can you guess what he does? He does a handstand – with his hat on! In fact he does lots of handstands. That's why people often call him 'Harry, the Happy Hat Man'.

Harry Hat Man   hen   hill   house

hay
Hats

Ink is interesting. Most of the words in books are printed with black ink and the pictures are printed with lots of different colours of ink. Inside each ink bottle there is usually only one colour but look at this ink bottle! Isn't it incredible?

Meet Impy Ink. He is an incredible ink bottle. Ink is like coloured water, so usually several colours in one bottle would get all mixed up and just look muddy. But Impy Ink has all seven colours of the rainbow inside him and none of them get mixed up.

Rainbow ink is Impy Ink's ingenious invention. Everyone insists, "It's impossible! It's incredible!" That's why people often call him 'Incredible Impy Ink'! Look at his incredible ink pen as well. It writes with rainbow ink!

Impy Ink   insect   invitation   ink

Who is this, jumping high in the air above Letterland?

Jumping Jim lives in a jigsaw house which he put together himself. Can you guess why he chose to live in a jigsaw house? It's because jigsaw begins with his sound! Ask Jumping Jim what he enjoys most and he will tell you, 'jumping and juggling'. Look at him juggling while he jumps! You can only ever see one of his juggling balls because the others are moving so fast.

Jumping Jim can jump as high as a jet plane in the sky. Sometimes he jumps so high that his head is hidden in the clouds. Can you see the picture on this page of Jumping Jim with his head in the clouds?

Jumping Jim   Jet   Jeep   jigsaw

Letterland's King is a keen football player. He loves kicking the ball really hard. That's why everybody calls him 'Kicking King'.

Kicking King is keen on his pets, too. He has a kangaroo, a koala and some very playful kittens. The kittens like to play with Kicking King's keys. When the King is not looking, they play with his kite as well, and get all tangled up!

All the Letterlanders love to play football with Kicking King. It looks like Noisy Nick is coming to play, too. Golden Girl is very good in goal. Do you think she is going to catch the ball or is the kangaroo going to kick it away?

Kicking King   **key**   **kite**   **kittens**

Everybody loves Lucy Lamp Light. This is because she has a lovely smile that lights everything around her in Letterland. All the animals gather round Lucy – even the lions and leopards – because they love her.

Lucy Lamp Light lives in the Letterland Lighthouse. At night, her light shines out from the lighthouse so that ships can find their way home. If anyone is lost or lonely, Lucy Lamp Light always helps them.

Sometimes Lucy Lamp Light helps out at the Letterland school. When it is time to go home in the winter her light shines brightly so the children can cross the road safely – even if it is dark or foggy.

Lucy Lamp Light   lemons   lamb   lion

Look! It's the marvellous metal monster, Munching Mike! At the moment he is munching on his main meal. It's a mixture of melon and mangos and marshmallows but he has mixed it in with bits of crunchy metal and magnets! Munching Mike lives in the mountains with his Mum. You can see her at the top of this page. The mountains are far away but that doesn't matter because Munching Mike and his Mum can move very quickly on their three metal wheels.

Many people think that monsters are scary, but Mike is the mildest monster you'll ever meet. Do you ever make his sound when you're munching on your favourite meal? 'Mmm…!'

Munching Mike   milk   moon   monkey

marshmallows

N

It is Noisy Nick's ninth birthday and he is very happy. His parents have given him a drum set so now he thinks he can make as much noise as he likes.

Nick loves making a noise. His neighbours think he is a nuisance because he loves hammering nails, and that is very noisy, too! Can you see how Nick has hammered together three of his nice new nails to make his capital letter at the top of this page?

Nick is having so much noisy fun at his birthday party that no one can hear anything! Perhaps he will be quiet for a few minutes so that Golden Girl can sing 'Happy Birthday'.

Can you find nine nails hidden in the picture?

Noisy Nick   nails   nest   nuts

Happy Birthday!

Oscar Orange lives at the Letterland docks. Every day, ships come to the docks bringing crates and boxes.

All sorts of things are unloaded at the Letterland docks: olives, otters and ostriches, and loads and loads of oranges. Oscar Orange has his hands full. Perhaps the octopus will help him. How many arms does he have?

Oscar Orange has a good old friend called Mr O who looks after him. He is the Old Man from over the ocean. No one knows exactly how old Mr O is, but the older he gets the wiser he becomes. Now he is the oldest and wisest man in Letterland.

Can you make Oscar Orange's nice, round orange shape with your mouth?

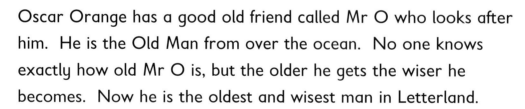

Oscar Orange   octopus   olives   otter

ORANGES

OLIVES

OTTAWA TRADERS
LAKE ONTARIO
CANADA

Peter Puppy loves playing in the park. He has lots of pals there.
Look at the penguins having fun on the slide. Peter Puppy thinks the
best time for playing in the park is just after it has been raining,
because then he can paddle in all the puddles. If it is a really hot
day, he likes to pop into the park pool with one of his puppy pals.

Peter loves to have picnics and parties in the park. He and his pals
eat peaches and pears and play pass-the-parcel. They always make
sure they leave some crumbs out for the pigeons and the parrot.

Can you see a present in the picture? Is it a present for Peter
Puppy? What do you think is inside it?

Peter Puppy   present   parrot   park

You might like to meet the Queen of Letterland, but don't talk to her right now. No one is allowed to say a word when the Queen is sitting quietly doing a quiz with her special quill pen.

If anyone dares to make a noise, the Queen will quarrel with them. She has had so many quarrels that now people call her 'Quarrelsome Queen'.

Look, there's the Queen's umbrella just behind her. She won't go anywhere in Letterland without her royal umbrella. If she loses it, she's sure to have a quarrel with someone! She even takes it with her when she goes to sit and rest in her special round Quiet Room. Can you see her in her Quiet Room at the top of this page?

Quarrelsome Queen   quilt   quiz   QUIET

Did you know there are robots in Letterland? This one is called Red Robot and he can be a trouble-maker. He likes to take things that don't belong to him and that's not right! He always carries a sack so he can put things in it and then roll away on his silver and red roller skates. No wonder people sometimes call him a robber robot!

Red Robot has a remote-control racing car. He'd better be careful or his racing car will run into the horses from the riding school.

Red Robot hopes you won't recognise him in his capital letter shape at the top of this page because the rascal has changed his shape. But we won't let him fool us, will we? We'll still hear him growling his 'rrr...' sound in words, whether he's big or small!

Red Robot radio robin rocket

'Sss…,' Sammy Snake is having a lovely time by the Letterland swimming pool. Sammy loves sun-bathing, but he is always careful to put on sun-cream when he's in the sun. The sun is so bright today he may even have to put on his sunhat and sunglasses, so he doesn't have to squint.

Sammy loves swimming too. He likes to splash in the sea or slide into the swimming pool. Afterwards, he has a sandwich and settles down to do some more sunbathing. All the splashing and sliding around has made Sammy quite sleepy. Soon he will be snoozing in the sun.

Who can you see splashing in the pool? Who's that on the sand by the sea?

Sammy Snake   **sun**   **sandwich**   **sea**

Talking Tess is always in a terrific hurry. This is because she is a very important person. She is in charge of all the telephones and televisions in Letterland. If anyone in Letterland has a problem with their telephone or television, they just get in touch with Talking Tess and she puts it right.

Tess talks on her mobile phone all the time. She keeps on talking when she travels in taxis or on trains, and even when she is having a cup of tea!

Sometimes Tess has to mend telephone wires high up in the sky. Then she does a very clever trick. She makes herself really tall. Can you see her at the top of this page with her head in the clouds?

Talking Tess   telephone   TAXI   train

U u

Look up in the sky and you might see Uppy Umbrella, a cheerful umbrella who lives in Letterland. Uppy loves to float up in the air. She doesn't even mind if she is blown upside down – unless she falls into her letter and gets stuck.

Uppy Umbrella loves it when it rains. She flies up, up, up and away, into the air with all her umbrella friends, waving at the people underneath. How many umbrellas can you see in this picture?

The person who looks after all the umbrellas in Letterland is Mr U, the Uniform Man. He has a very useful job. He has to make sure everyone has an umbrella when it rains. Especially Quarrelsome Queen!

Uppy Umbrella   up   upside down

Vicky Violet loves flowers, especially violets because they have lovely velvet leaves and petals. Vicky's violets are very special too, because they have faces – and they talk! Can you guess what they say? They make the 'vvv…' sound at the start of Vicky Violet's name. Vicky keeps these violets in a very big, very valuable vase where they have grown roots so they can go on living there.

Vicky lives in a village in the Letterland valley where they grow lots of vegetables as well as flowers. How many different vegetables can you see in this picture?

Can you see a very big bird? That's Vernon Vulture. What is that in his beak? Perhaps it's a valentine card for Vicky Violet...

Vicky Violet   Vase   Village   Volcano

Whenever you're near water in Letterland, you can be sure that Walter Walrus will be wallowing close by. Walter Walrus loves to rest with his webbed flippers wedged into his two water wells while he sunbathes. Walter likes to watch the whales splashing in the water, making huge, white waves.

The whales are not the only ones making waves in Letterland though. When you go near Walter, be wary. At times he gets quite wild. He whips up waves in his water wells. Then, SPLASH! You will get all wet!

Everyone in Letterland enjoys Walter Walrus, except when he teases them by splashing them all over with his salty water. Then they wish he was anywhere else in the world, but not in Letterland!

 Walter Walrus   water   whale   windmill

"Relax," said Max to his friend Maxine, "while I fix this box for our pet fox." Maxine is happy because Max has already fixed her deckchair for her. Max enjoys fixing things so much that the Letterlanders call him Fix-it Max. Next he is going to fix Eddy Elephant's broken exercise machine, and after that Eddy has left him a broken Exit sign to fix.

Max has lots of tools, but he knows never to touch dangerous things like saws unless there is a grown-up there.

Max always gives things back with a little note saying,

> All fixed!
> Love and xxx,
> Max

Fix-it Max   box   fox   EXIT

If you like yo-yos, then you will like the Yellow Yo-yo Man. He has been selling yo-yos for years, but he still needs to sell lots more. That is because he is saving up to buy a yacht, like the one with yellow sails in the picture, and yachts cost a lot of money.

So, if you went to Letterland, it wouldn't be long before you would hear Yo-yo Man yelling, "Yo-yos for sale! Super yyyellow yo-yos!" Then you would see him showing the children how to yank the yo-yos to make them climb up and down on their strings, just like he is doing in this picture.

Do you like yo-yos? Yes! Would you like one of Yellow Yo-yo Man's yo-yos, too?

Yellow Yo-yo Man   yacht   yellow   yolk

Zig Zag Zebra is going for a quick canter around the Letterland Zoo. She doesn't usually stop to chat because she is so shy. She would rather just zoom by.

The Letterland zoo is a very special zoo because the animals are so friendly. You will often see a giraffe or a lion strolling around together. But you might like to close your eyes when Zig Zag Zebra crosses at a zebra crossing. Otherwise you could get quite dizzy looking at all the black and white stripes!

Did you know that Zig Zag Zebra is the fastest runner in Letterland? Well she is. She has won zillions of prizes. When she gets tired of zooming around the zoo, she settles down for a snooze and falls fast asleep. Zzzzzz.

Zig Zag Zebra   dizzy   zoo   snooze

There are five very important men in Letterland, the Vowel Men. You have already met Mr A, the Apron Man and Mr E. Everyone calls Mr E the Easy Magic Man because, unlike you and me, he finds doing magic tricks eeeasy! Next comes Mr I, the Ice Cream Man, who sells very fine ice cream. Mr I also looks after Impy Ink. You have seen Old Mr O from over the ocean in a boat (behind Oscar Orange at the docks), and Mr U, the Uniform Man who looks after all the umbrellas in Letterland.

Everyone in Letterland makes a special sound when they go in words – but not the five Vowel Men! They are the only Letterlanders that ever say their names in words – A! E! I! O! U!
Listen out for them. You'll hear them every day.

apron   easy   ice cream   ocean   uniform

How to use this Letterland book

The *Letterland ABC* is designed for you to share with your children. They will think of it all as simply fun, but with your help, they'll be learning important first reading, speaking and listening skills.

To start with, look for all the objects that start with the same sound as the featured Letterlander. The **a-z** lists below include most, but not all of them!

Play with letter sounds. Decide what the Letterlanders would like to eat, drink, do. Accept all answers, but give special praise for answers beginning with the Letterlander's sound, for example, bread and butter for Bouncy Ben, carrot cake for Clever Cat. Would Firefighter Fred prefer a cup of cocoa or a fresh fruit drink?

Have fun talking about where the objects are and let your child decide might happen next. For example, do you think the helicopter will land on the hillside so the pilot can buy a hat from Harry Hat Man's shop?

On a second or third read, you could ask your child to tell you all about each picture. Listen carefully as your child points out all the objects that start with the featured sounds, and tells you what is going on in each picture.

A	B	bulrushes	cockerel	doll	entrance	foam	greenhouse
acrobat	ball	bushes	cocoa	donkey	EXIT	forest	
alligator	balloon	buttercups	cow	door		fox	H
animals	basket	butterflies	crocus	dragonfly	F	frogs	hat
ankles	bat		crossword	duckpond	farm		hay
ant	bee	C	crows	duckweed	fawn	G	hedge
anteater	blackberries	cake	cucumber		fence	garden	hedgehogs
antelope	bluebells	calf		E	fern	geese	helicopter
apple	bluetits	car	D	eclairs	finch	gladioli	hen
apple trees	boat	carnations	daffodil	edges	fir trees	glass	hill
arrow	book	castle	daisy	eggs	fire engine	glasses	hives
astronaut	box	caterpillar	deer	elbows	flags	grapes	home
atlas	bridge	clover	dinosaur	elephant	flames	grass	horse
axe	brothers	clouds	dog	emerald	flowers	green	house

hut
hydrangea

I
iguana
India
indigo
ink
ink pen
insect
invention
invitation
Italy

J
jacket
jasmine
jay
jeep
jet
jigsaw
jockey
juggling balls
juniper

K
kangaroo
kennel
kestrel
kettle
key

kingfisher
kite
kittens
koala

L
ladder
lemons
leopard
light
lighthouse
lilies
lion
lion cub
lizard
llama
lobster
locket
logs
lorry

M
magnet
mango
marshmallows
melon
metal
midnight
milk
millipede
monkey

moon
moth
mountains
mouse
mushrooms

N
nails
neck
necklace
needle
nest
nine
noise
nuts

O
octopus
olives
on
orange
oranges
ostrich
otter

P
palm tree
park
parrot
path
peaches

pears
penguins
pigeons
pine cones
pink
playground
pool
poppies
present
puddle
purple

Q
quail
queen
question mark
QUIET
quill
quilt
quince
quiz

R
racoon
rainbow
recorder
red
riding school
rings
robins
rocket

roller skates
roses
rubbish
ruby ring
ruler

S
sail boat
sand
sandwiches
satsuma
saucer
sea
seagull
sky
stars
strawberry
sun
sun cream
sundae
sunglasses
sunhat
swimming-
pool

T
TAXI
teddy
telephone
terrace
toad

toes
towers
train
trees
tricycle
tug boat
tulips
two

U
umbrellas
upside down

V
valentine card
vegetable
verbena
village
vinegar
violets
violin
volcano
vole
vulture

W
wasp
water
waterfall
waves
weasel

whales
whiskers
white
windmill
window
wolf
wombat
woodpecker

X
box
exercise
machine
EXIT sign
Fix-it sign
fox
Maxine

Y
yacht
yak
yellow
yoghurt
yolk
yorkies
yo-yos

Z
zebra
zoo

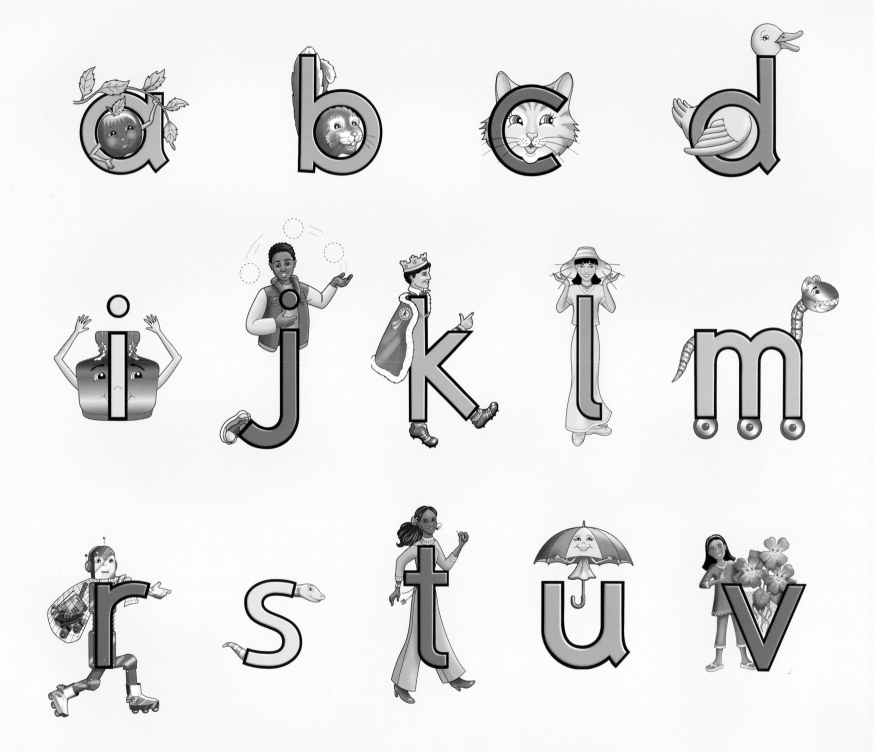

More from Letterland

The Letterland system teaches all 44 letter sounds in the English language through stories rather than rules. There are resources to take children from the very first stages of learning to full literacy.

Beyond ABC is the second in the set of three books, which together hold vital keys to learning to read. Beautifully illustrated, it opens up the secrets of 22 major spelling patterns.

Collect the set

ABC Book

Beyond ABC

Far Beyond ABC

See our full range at www.letterland.com

Activity Books

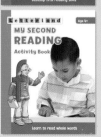

Flashcards

Software

First Picture Word Book

Alphabet of Rhymes

Bedtime Stories

Alphabet Adventures

Story Books